PUFFIN BOOKS

GERBIL CRAZY!

All Sarah's friends have pets of one sort or another, but Sarah has never been really interested in animals. Until the day her best friend's gerbil has babies. As soon as Sarah sees the smallest one, she knows she has to have it. At first, her parents are totally against the whole idea, but she soon changes their minds and the new gerbil is named Georgie. But Georgie has a terrible habit – he keeps running away. This is bad enough at home, but when Sarah disobeys orders and takes Georgie to school, chaos breaks out.

Tony Bradman was born in London. After graduating from Cambridge in 1976, he worked in the music business but moved rapidly into publishing. A former deputy editor of *Parents* magazine, in 1980 he launched the *Parents* Best Books for Babies award. He has done much to promote children's books generally and has himself written fiction and poetry for children and edited several anthologies. He lives with his wife and three children in Kent.

Tony Bradman

Gerbil Crazy!

Illustrated by Shelagh McNicholas

PUFFIN BOOKS

PUFFIN BOOKS

Published by the Penguin Group
Penguin Books Ltd, 27 Wrights Lane, London W8 5TZ, England
Viking Penguin, a division of Penguin Books USA Inc.
375 Hudson Street, New York, New York 10014, USA
Penguin Books Australia Ltd, Ringwood, Victoria, Australia
Penguin Books Canada Ltd, 2801 John Street, Markham, Ontario, Canada L3R 1B4
Penguin Books (NZ) Ltd, 182–190 Wairau Road, Auckland 10, New Zealand

Penguin Books Ltd, Registered Offices: Harmondsworth, Middlesex, England

First published by Viking 1990
Published in Puffin Books 1991
10 9 8 7 6 5 4 3 2 1

For Nicole Lauren
– we're all Nicole crazy!

Chapter One

"**M**um, can I have a gerbil?"
Sarah knew what her mum's
answer would be, even before she
asked the question.

"Certainly not," she said.

"They're like mice, aren't they? I'm not having little furry creatures running around the house. Yuck!"

"I only want *one* gerbil, Mum," said Sarah. "And it wouldn't do any running around. It would be in a cage."

They turned the corner into

their street. The car was
parked by the gate, which meant
Dad was already at home.

"Anyway, what's brought all
this on?" asked Sarah's mum.
"You've never asked for a pet
before."

Sarah didn't say anything,
but it was true. Most of her

9

friends had pets of one sort or
another. But she'd never really
been interested in animals . . .
until today.

Sarah always went round to
play with her best friend Lisa
Brown after school on Mondays.
Then Mum collected her on the
way home from work.

Lisa was lots of fun. Usually

they played with some of Lisa's toys, or watched TV together. But today Lisa had been too excited to play. She had two gerbils – and one of them had just had babies!

Lisa wanted to keep them all, but her mum said she couldn't. So they would have to find new homes for them.

There were five babies altogether; five tiny, pink creatures snuggled up beside their mother. As soon as Sarah had seen the smallest one, she knew she wanted him more than she'd ever wanted anything else in her life.

They walked up the garden path to the front door. Sarah's mum opened it with her key.

"Hello!" she called out. "Is dinner ready yet?"

"Give us a chance," said Sarah's dad, as he came out of the kitchen. "I've only just got in myself. Hello, Sarah love. Why the long face?"

"Your daughter wants a gerbil, of all things," said Sarah's mum. "And I've said no."

"This wouldn't have anything to do with the fact that one of Lisa Brown's gerbils has just had babies, would it?" asked

Sarah's dad. "I saw her dad in town today."

"Ah, now I understand," said Sarah's mum.

"Lisa's mum won't let her keep all the babies," said Sarah. "She said I could have the smallest one if I wanted. Can I?"

"We'll talk about it later," said Dad. "If we don't get on with the dinner, none of us will get anything to eat tonight, and I'm starving."

Sarah decided she wasn't going to give up. She wanted that gerbil, and she was determined to have him. So, as

soon as they'd finished dinner,
she asked again.

Her mum and dad talked about
it for a long time . . . a very
long time. They went on, and on,
and on, and on. And just when
Sarah thought they had finished,
they started going on, and on,
and on, and on, again. Sarah

couldn't get a word in at all.

"But I really don't like the idea, Sarah," her mum said. "It would always remind me of mice . . . and don't they smell? Your Auntie Jenny used to have a rabbit, and the hutch smelt awful." She wrinkled up her nose.

"I don't think gerbils smell all that much," said Dad. "You do have to clean out the cage, though, and I definitely don't want to do that. Who's going to remember to feed the poor animal, too? I know what you're like, Sarah. You'd forget your own head if it wasn't

attached to your neck . . ."

After ten minutes of this, Sarah felt as if she was going to explode. But then she got her chance – they actually stopped talking for a second. Before they could interrupt her, she said that *she* would feed the gerbil, *and* clean out the cage. She promised she wouldn't ever forget.

Sarah's mum and dad looked at each other.

"We'll have to buy a cage, I suppose," Mum said.

"I'll help pay for it," said Sarah. "I've saved up some of my pocket money."

"We can't really say no then, can we?" said her dad with a smile.

Sarah smiled back.

The smallest baby gerbil wouldn't be old enough to leave his mother for a couple of weeks, so Sarah had to wait. In the mean time, they bought a

cage, a food bowl, and a water
bottle with a tube. They even
bought a little plastic house
for him to sleep in.

It was all perfect. Finally,
the day came when Sarah went
with her mum and dad to collect
her new pet. She had a name
ready for him, too.

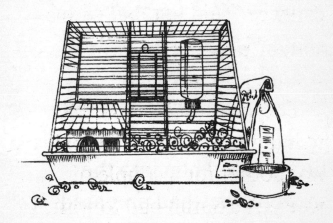

"Hello, Georgie," she said, as Lisa popped him into the shoebox they had prepared. It had tissue inside, and some

small holes in the lid so that
he could breathe.

Sarah held the shoebox very
carefully all the way home.

23

When they arrived they went straight into the front room, where Georgie's cage was waiting for him. Sarah put the shoebox down, lifted its lid, and put in her hand.

"Be careful, Sarah," said her mum. Sarah looked round at her.

Just then, Georgie ran up her arm, jumped off her shoulder on to the floor, and disappeared under an armchair.

Sarah's mum screamed.

Chapter Two

It took them nearly two hours
to catch Georgie. Sarah's mum
wouldn't help. She just sat on
an armchair with her legs
tucked up beneath her. She held

a cushion over her feet, and
kept telling Dad and Sarah
where to look.

"It must have gone under the
sofa," she shouted. "No! No!
There it is – quick, Jim.
Quick!"

Sarah's dad dived to the floor, but he missed Georgie completely.

"Blast!" he said. "Sarah, you go to that end of the sofa, and I'll wait here."

They tried everything they could think of, and Sarah's dad did lots of diving and jumping

and running around. He made lots of noise, too. Sarah thought it was all a bit daft, really.

"He's only running away because he's scared," she said, "and we're making him more scared than ever."

"Well, clever clogs," said her dad, "have you got any ideas? He's supposed to be your pet, after all."

Sarah didn't have any ideas, but she was the one who caught Georgie in the end. One of her wellies was lying on its side by the back door, and she saw him go scampering into it.

She quietly took an empty

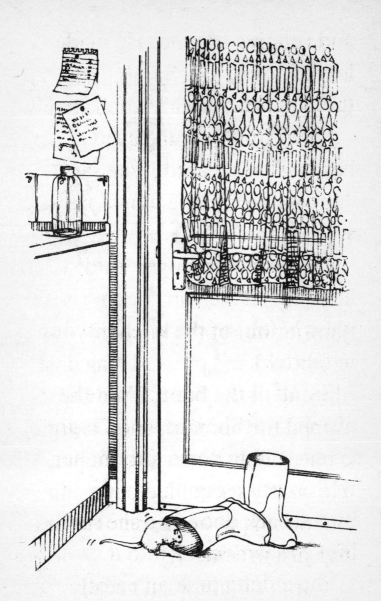

jam-jar out of the kitchen
cupboard and pressed it against
the end of the boot. Then she
tipped the boot up, and Georgie
came rolling down into the jar.
He nearly scrambled out again,
but Sarah put her hand over the
top just in time.

Sarah's mum wasn't really

happy until Georgie was in his
cage, and for a while it looked
as if he might be going
straight back to Lisa's house.
But Sarah begged and pleaded,
and in the end her mum said he
could stay.

"He won't get out again, Mum,"
said Sarah. "I promise."

Georgie did behave himself –
for a while. Sarah got to know
him very well. She filled his
bowl with food and changed his
water. She gave him the
cardboard tubes from the inside
of toilet rolls to play with
and chew. She gave him loads of
tissue to tear up and make
nests in.

She also spent lots of time
just gazing at him through the
bars of his cage. It wasn't
long before he was staring back
at her.

Sometimes she put her finger
between the bars, and he would
give it a soft little nibble.

Once, Sarah put her face very close to the cage. Georgie stood up on his hind legs and sniffed at her nose. It tickled – it felt as if he was giving her a kiss.

Sarah laughed. She was so pleased, she decided to take him out for a cuddle.

She opened the cage and put her hand in. Georgie sniffed at her fingers, then scrambled over her hand and through the door. Sarah tried to pull her hand out, but it was stuck. She looked over her shoulder just in time to see Georgie running out of the bedroom.

Seconds later, Sarah could hear somebody shouting. At first she thought it was her mum, but it wasn't. It was Mr Peters, their elderly next-door neighbour. When Sarah got downstairs, she saw Mr Peters standing on the sofa, next to Mum. Both of them were looking down at Georgie on the floor.

"Sarah," her mum said. "Do something!"

At least it didn't take too long to catch him. Sarah had Georgie in her jam-jar within half an hour. But Mum was still very cross.

"Poor old Mr Peters!" she

said. "He was so worried. He was convinced it was a rat, Jim. It took me ages to persuade him it was just a gerbil."

"More like a greyhound," said Sarah's dad. "That gerbil can move pretty quickly. You'll just have to be more careful, Sarah."

Sarah promised she wouldn't let Georgie escape again.

But Georgie didn't promise not to try. Over the next few weeks, it seemed that every time Sarah opened the cage door to change his food, or put some tissue in, Georgie was off and

running as fast as his little
legs could carry him.

He took to hiding in some
very strange places, too. He
turned up inside the teapot one
day, just as Mum was about to
fill it with boiling water. She
said it was quite a shock when
she saw his head pop up.

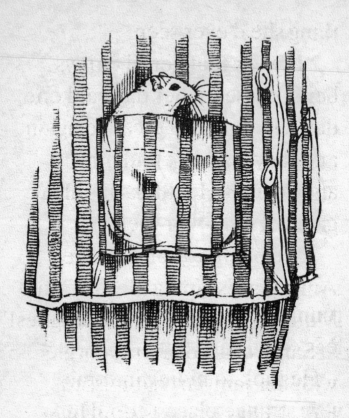

Then Dad had a surprise when
Georgie appeared in his pyjama
pocket early one Sunday morning.
Sarah's mum said the look on
Dad's face was the funniest

thing she'd ever seen.

"I swear that gerbil enjoys being chased," her dad said one day. Georgie had escaped again, and they couldn't find him anywhere. "He thinks it's all a game of hide-and-seek."

"We ought to call him the Amazing Escaping Gerbil," said Mum. "Look out! There he goes!"

Sarah chased after Georgie with her jam-jar, but missed him. They chased him all over the house, clambering over furniture, rushing in and out of rooms. Dad broke one of Mum's favourite vases, and Sarah spilt a whole mug of coffee on an armchair. Dad said the stain would never come out.

It took them three hours to catch him this time. It was Georgie's longest escape ever.

He can't do anything worse than this, thought Sarah, as she put him back in his cage.

But Georgie could, as Sarah soon found out.

Chapter Three

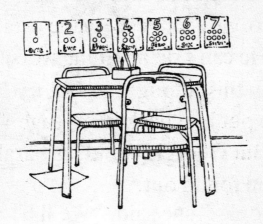

A few days later, Sarah's teacher, Mrs Beattie, told the class she wanted them to work on a new topic.

"We'll call it Animals and

People," she said. "We'll be
looking at how people and
animals live and work together.
We'll start with pets today.
Now, who's going to tell us
about their pet?"

Lots of hands went up, and
one by one Sarah's class talked

about the animals they had at
home. Soon it was Sarah's turn,
and she told everyone about
Georgie.

"Please, Miss," said Neil
Stanton, "what does a gerbil
look like?"

"They're small and usually

brown or black, aren't they, Sarah?" said Mrs Beattie. Sarah nodded. "I haven't got a picture of one. But perhaps if we ask Sarah nicely, she'll bring Georgie in to meet us tomorrow. Will you do that, Sarah?"

Sarah nodded again. She thought it was a terrific idea.

Mum, however, didn't think it was a very good idea at all.

It was the first thing Sarah asked when Mum picked her up from school.

"I'm sorry, Sarah, but the answer's no," she said. "You know what Georgie's like. If he

escapes at school, you might
never find him again."

Sarah hadn't thought about
that. But she was sure Georgie
wouldn't try to get away at
school, and she wanted to take
him *so* much.

"I'll be extra careful with

him, Mum, I promise," she said.

"The answer's still no, Sarah."

"But, Mum –"

"No 'buts' about it, Sarah," said Mum. "You're not taking Georgie with you to school, and that's *that*."

Later, at home, Sarah sat in her bedroom sulking. She looked

at Georgie in his cage.

"It's not fair, is it, Georgie?" she said. Georgie stood on his hind legs and stared at her.

Then Sarah had an idea – a brilliant idea. She was going to take Georgie to school and bring him back without telling Mum and Dad. They would never know. She just had to plan it properly!

By the time she got up the next morning, she had it all worked out. There was a zip-up pocket in her coat. She could slip Georgie into it before Dad took her to school.

She just had to put on her
coat, then pop upstairs to her
bedroom before they left. And
that's exactly what she did.

Sarah dashed into her bedroom
and knelt down by Georgie's
cage. "Now be a good boy,
Georgie," she said, as she

opened the door. She certainly
didn't want him to escape now!

"Come on, Sarah! What are
you doing? We'll be late!" It
was her dad, calling from
downstairs.

"Coming!" Sarah called back, as
she popped Georgie into her

pocket and zipped it up. "Phew!"
she said to herself quietly,
and went down to the front door.

Dad was already in the car.
Sarah picked up her lunchbox,
kissed Mum goodbye, dashed
outside, and got into the car.

"You get slower and slower in
the mornings, Sarah," her dad
said as he drove off. "And
what's wrong with you now? Why
are you wriggling about like
that? You look as if you've got
ants in your pants!"

"Sorry, Dad," said Sarah. She
tried to stop wriggling, but it
was very difficult. Georgie was
climbing round and round inside

her coat pocket. He was
tickling her so much, she could
hardly stop herself from
laughing out loud.

Dad dropped her off at school,
and Sarah ran into the
playground. The teacher on
playground duty had already
blown the whistle, so everyone

was going into the school.
Sarah followed her class, but
she didn't take her coat off
and hang it up in the cloakroom.

Instead, she went straight
into the classroom and up to
Mrs Beattie, who was sitting
at her desk.

"Good morning, Sarah," she

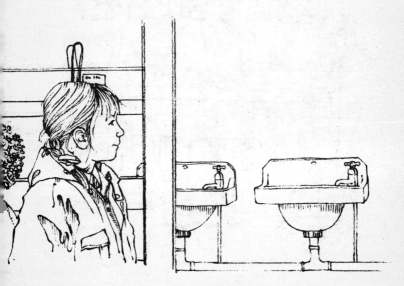

said. "Why haven't you taken
your coat off?"

Sarah didn't say anything.
She carefully unzipped her coat
pocket, reached in, and took
Georgie out. She held him

tightly, but as gently as she could, and lifted him up for Mrs Beattie to see.

"Ah," said Mrs Beattie, "this must be Georgie. I wish you'd brought him *in* something, Sarah, but never mind. I think we've got a box somewhere, haven't we?"

Mrs Beattie found a plastic box the class had kept some stick insects in. She said the sides were too high and slippery for Georgie to climb up. Sarah put him in it.

The classroom was filling up, and everyone was making lots of noise.

"Right, Class Five!" shouted
Mrs Beattie. "Settle down. We've
got a special visitor today,
but he's very small so you'll
have to gather round."

Mrs Beattie got the class to
sit on the floor in the reading
corner. She put the box in
front of them.

"Say hello to Georgie,

everyone," she said. The class said hello. Neil Stanton was sitting at the front. He leant forward and tipped the plastic box towards him.

"Don't do that, Neil," said Mrs Beattie.

But it was too late.

Georgie scampered on to his hand, up his arm, jumped on to the floor, and ran off as fast as his little legs could carry him.

Georgie had escaped!

Chapter Four

Sarah tried to catch Georgie,
but it was impossible. He ran
all around the classroom, in
and out of the children's legs,
under the tables and chairs,

even over Mrs Beattie's feet.
Everyone was screaming and
running around and knocking
things over. Mrs Beattie got

more and more cross.

"Children, children!" she
shouted. "Will you *please* sit
down. We'll never catch him at

this rate! Quick, Sarah, he's gone behind the bookstand. I'll try to cut off his way out."

Just at that moment, the door opened.

"What on earth is going on in here?" It was Mrs Smith, the headteacher. "We can hear the noise all over the school!"

Mrs Beattie opened her mouth to say something, but she never got the chance. Georgie ran out from behind the bookstand and dashed across the classroom. Then he shot out of the door, right past Mrs Smith.

Mrs Smith, looking very surprised, jumped back. Sarah

ran out of the classroom and
saw Georgie scampering down the
corridor. He was keeping close
to the wall. Soon he came to
Class Six's door, which was
open.

Sarah saw him stop, sit up on
his hind legs, and look through

the doorway. But before she could reach him, he'd made his

mind up and run in. Then she heard lots of shouting and yelling.

Nobody could catch Georgie. He caused the same uproar in Class Six as he had in Class

Five. When he'd finished running around in there, he escaped through the door and got into Class Seven. Then he disappeared. But not for long.

Every so often during the rest of the morning, Sarah heard screams coming from somewhere in the school. She knew it was Georgie turning up, but by the time she and Mrs Beattie got there, he'd gone again.

They did see him once more, though. They were going past Mrs Smith's office, when Mrs Beattie saw him by the door to the hall.

"Quick, Sarah, there he is!"
she shouted, and ran off. Mrs
Smith came out of her office
and followed after them. Sarah
had never seen teachers run
about so much.

But Georgie got away again.

Sarah was beginning to think
that they would never find

him – and what was she going to say to her mum and dad if he didn't turn up? She could feel her eyes beginning to prickle. She felt like crying all the time.

At morning play, Mrs Beattie went with Sarah to ask Mr Barnes, the caretaker, if he would help them look for Georgie.

"A runaway gerbil, you say," he said, rubbing his chin. "He could be anywhere. I just hope that big old cat who's been hanging around the playground doesn't get to him before we do."

Sarah burst into tears.

They searched everywhere at lunchtime. The whole of Class Five helped, and some of the teachers, too. But it was no good. No one saw any sign of him.

Georgie had completely disappeared.

Sarah felt really miserable as she sat in the hall eating her sandwiches. Her lunchbox was lying open under the table. She thought about Georgie, and almost started crying again.

Then suddenly she felt something tickling her feet. She peered down at them, but

couldn't see anything unusual.
She was just about to have a
proper look, when Mrs Beattie
came over to her.

"Never mind, Sarah," she said.
"I'm sure we'll find him before
home-time."

But there were no screams,
and no gerbil chases in the
afternoon. At the end of school,

Mrs Beattie came out with
Sarah to talk to her mum.

She explained what had
happened, and said that Georgie
would probably turn up
eventually. She didn't look as
if she meant it, though. Mum
didn't say anything to Mrs
Beattie, but Sarah could see
she was very cross.

"Well, young lady," she said, as she put Sarah's lunchbox on the kitchen table. "You've only got yourself to blame. I don't like to say I told you so . . ."

She told Sarah off, and went on, and on, and on. Then, just when Sarah thought she'd finished, she started going on, and on, and on, and on, again.

Sarah burst into tears again.

After that, her mum was quite nice. She made Sarah a drink and a snack, and said she wasn't to worry. "Mrs Beattie will find him, you wait and see."

Sarah didn't think so. She

sat in her bedroom, staring at
Georgie's empty cage.

A little later, her dad came
home.

"Hello, everyone!" he called
out, as he came through the
door. "What's for dinner? I'm
starving!"

"Jim, something's happened . . ."

Sarah heard her mum say. Dad
didn't seem to take any notice.
He walked straight into the
kitchen.

"Hey, haven't you got the
dinner going yet?" Sarah heard
him say. "You haven't even
emptied Sarah's lunchbox!"

The next thing Sarah heard

was a yell of surprise, and her dad shouting, "What the –"

Sarah dashed downstairs and opened the kitchen door. As she did so, a small brown shape shot past her and into the front room.

It was Georgie!

"He was in your lunchbox, Sarah," shouted Dad as he ran past her. "He jumped out when I opened it!" So that was why her feet had been tickly in the hall at lunchtime!

Sarah followed her dad into
the front room. They spent ages
chasing Georgie, but they
didn't really mind. They were
just pleased to have him home.
Even Mum looked relieved.

And a little later, Sarah had

an idea. A *really* brilliant idea, this time.

"Mum," she said, "do you think Georgie wouldn't try to escape so much if he had a friend to play with?"

Sarah knew the answer before she'd even finished asking the question.

"You want us to have *another* gerbil?" said her mum. "Look out, Jim, he's behind you – mind that lamp! Certainly not, Sarah. What's come over you? You must be gerbil crazy!"

Sarah smiled. Her mum was right, she *was* gerbil crazy. Now, where was that jam-jar . . .